I0805912

curious about

TENNIS

BY KRISSY EBERTH

AMICUS LEARNING

What are you

curious about?

CHAPTER THREE

3

Playing the Game

Curious About is published
by Amicus Learning,
an imprint of Amicus
P.O. Box 227
Mankato, MN 56002
www.amicuspublishing.us

Editor: Grace Cain and Megan Siewert
Series Designer: Kathleen Petelinsek
Book Designer and Photo Researcher: Emily Dietz

Library of Congress Cataloging-in-Publication Data
Names: Eberth, Kristin, author.
Title: Curious about tennis / by Krissy Eberth. Description: Mankato, Minnesota : Amicus Learning, 2025. | Series: Curious about sports | Includes bibliographical references and index. | Audience: Ages 5-9 | Audience: Grades 2-3 | Summary: "Conversational questions and answers share what kids can expect when they join tennis, including what gear to pack, types of tennis strokes, and how scoring works. A Stay Curious! feature models research skills while simple infographics support visual literacy. Includes glossary and index"– Provided by publisher.
Identifiers: LCCN 2023043291 (print) | LCCN 2023043292 (ebook) | ISBN 9781645497127 (library binding) | ISBN 9781681529752 (paperback) | ISBN 9781645497189 (ebook)
Subjects: LCSH: Tennis–Juvenile literature.
Classification: LCC GV996.5 .E34 2025 (print) | LCC GV996.5 (ebook) | DDC 796.342–dc23/eng/20230929 LC record available at https://lccn.loc.gov/2023043291 LC ebook record available at https://lccn.loc.gov/2023043292

Photo Credits: Adobe Stock/Павел Мещеряков, 3, 20–21; Depositphotos/Xalanx, Cover, 1; Getty/Cavan Images / Robert Niedring photographer, 10–11, Johner Images, 4–5; iStock/Arturo Peña Romano Medina, 2, 7, ChrisGorgio, 13, Harbucks, 8, Machacekcz, 15, Maksym Rudoi, 7, max-kegfire, 17, microgen, 12, nd3000, 2, 15, pixdeluxe, 9, YakobchukOlena, 19; Noun Project/Kido Chang, 22, 23, vectonator, 22, 23; Shutterstock/cirkoglu, 16

CHAPTER ONE

Who can play tennis?

Anyone can! Boys and girls can both play tennis. Most programs have group lessons based on age. There are even classes for toddlers and grandparents. Many players start at about six years old.

You can play tennis with any of your friends or family.

What gear do I need?

Grab a racket and tennis balls. Make sure your racket is the right size for your age and ability. This helps you swing the racket correctly. You'll also want tennis shoes. They make it safer to run around the court.

All you need to get started is a pair of tennis shoes, a racket, and tennis balls.

PICK THE RIGHT RACKET

19 inches (48 centimeters)	21 in (53 cm)	23 in (58 cm)	25 in (64 cm)	27 in (68 cm)
Ages 2–4	Ages 4–6	Ages 6–8	Ages 8–11	Ages 12 +

Using a wall to practice is a good way to improve your skills.

Where do I practice?

You can play tennis at your local park or community center.

Anywhere! You can practice against a wall or on a driveway. Your lessons will be on a court. Many outdoor courts have lights. These let you play at night. You can also practice inside at a gym or indoor court.

CHAPTER TWO

What team can I play on?

Younger kids can join a local club team. When you are ready, you can compete in **tournaments**. Your coach will help you prepare for the **matches.** Once you get older, you can join your school's tennis team. You'll play against kids from other schools.

You can join a local tennis club team and play with kids your age.

Practicing with a step platform can help improve your footwork.

What will I learn at practice?

Your coach will teach you different **strokes**. You will also practice running and moving your feet. This is called **footwork**. It helps you move towards the ball faster. Tennis takes coordination and speed.

TYPES OF TENNIS STROKES

SERVE
A shot to start a point.

BACKHAND
When the palm of the hand holding the racket is turned in the opposite direction to the ball.

FOREHAND
When the palm of the hand holding the racket is turned in the direction of the ball.

OVERHEAD
When you hit the ball above your head.

GROUNDSTROKE
When you hit the ball after it bounces once.

VOLLEY
When you hit the ball before it bounces.

Who will I play with?

Other kids your age. You'll play with kids at the same skill level. You can play **singles** or **doubles**. In singles, one person plays against the other. In doubles, there are teams of two. One team plays on each side of the net.

Mixed doubles are teams of two that have one boy and one girl.

DID YOU KNOW?
The lines on the court show you where to aim the ball. Singles and doubles have different lines.

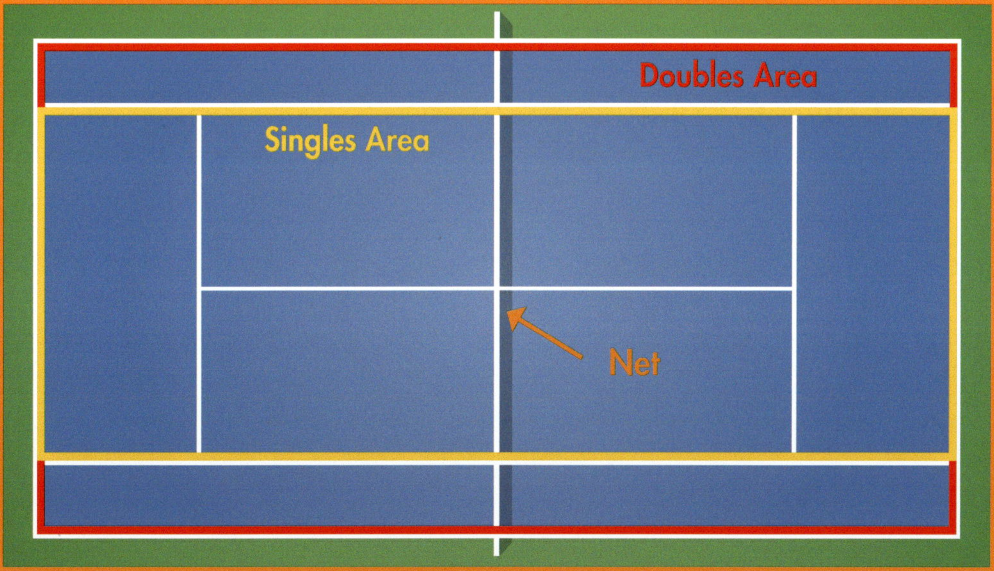

CHAPTER THREE

3

Do I hit the ball as hard as I can?

A player gets ready to swing his racket.

No. It might be fun to swing hard. But good tennis players are always in control of the ball. You have to aim carefully to get a point. Tennis players use angles, spin, and speed on their shots. Sometimes, a sneaky, short shot wins the point!

DID YOU KNOW?

A mistake on a serve is called a **fault**. The server gets another try. If they make another mistake, the other player gets a point.

To serve the ball, lightly toss the ball into the air and swing your racket. Don't forget to aim!

How does the scoring work?

Players **rally** until one person fails to hit the ball back over the net. Then the other person gets a point. Tennis uses weird scoring. The first point is called 15. Then you get 30 for the second point and 40 for the third point. The fourth point is a win. You need to win by two points. If you are tied at 40, the game keeps going until someone wins by two.

Keeping your eye on the ball can help with coordination.

SCORING IN TENNIS

NUMBER OF POINTS	TERM
0	Love
1	15
2	30
3	40
4	Win

How many games do I play?

DID YOU KNOW?
A beginner match may last 20 minutes. Pro matches can last hours. You need endurance to be able to play a long match.

Quite a few! You need to win at least six games to win a **set**. And you need to win by two games. If you are tied at six games each, you will play a tiebreaker game. The number of sets in each match depends on your skill level. Most matches have three to five sets. If you win the most sets, you win the match!

Tennis players need to move quickly to hit the ball from both sides of the court.

STAY CURIOUS!

ASK MORE QUESTIONS

How do I know if I play right-handed or left-handed?

How do I find a doubles partner?

Try a BIG QUESTION: How does tennis help me stay healthy?

SEARCH FOR ANSWERS

Search the library catalog or the Internet.
A librarian, teacher, or parent can help you.

Using Keywords
Find the looking glass.

Keywords are the most important words in your question.

If you want to know about:

- how you know if you play right-handed or left-handed, type: TENNIS HANDEDNESS
- how to find a doubles partner, type: FIND TENNIS DOUBLES PARTNER

LEARN MORE

FIND GOOD SOURCES

Here are some good, safe sources you can use in your research.
Your librarian can help you find more.

Books

The Science of Tennis
by Emilie Dufresne, 2020.

Tennis
by Kara L. Laughlin, 2023.

Internet Sites

Tennis
https://kids.britannica.com/kids/article/tennis/353847
This site provides a kid-friendly introduction to information about playing tennis and the history of the sport.

Tennis Facts for Kids
https://kids.kiddle.co/Tennis
This site provides information about how to play tennis, professional competitions to watch, and images to introduce kids to the sport.

Every effort has been made to ensure that these websites are appropriate for children. However, because of the nature of the Internet, it is impossible to guarantee that these sites will remain active indefinitely or that their contents will not be altered.

SHARE AND TAKE ACTION

Hit a tennis ball against a wall outside.
Practice aiming at different spots on the wall.

Go with a friend to a tennis court near you.
See how long you can continue a rally.

Watch a tennis match at a club near you.
Watch the players rally to help you learn new tennis strokes.

GLOSSARY

doubles Four people playing at once, with two on each side playing as a team.

fault When a player makes a mistake on a serve.

footwork Moving your feet to get to the ball.

match A full competition in tennis.

rally When two players hit the ball back and forth over the net and inside the lines.

serve Starting a rally by being the first to hit a ball over the net to an opponent.

set At least six games played in a row; a player must win by two games to win a set.

singles Two people playing against each other, one on each side of the net.

stroke Hitting a tennis ball with a tennis racket.

tournament A competition that involves many players, often held over several days.

INDEX

About the Author

Krissy Eberth loves being active, especially playing tennis with her husband and daughters. When away from her writing desk, she can be found skiing, hiking, or biking the trails of northern Minnesota.